This book is dedicated
to the love of my life, Micah Marshall,
and my family, who support, love,
and pray for us faithfully.

WHEN WE **PRAY,** IT'S LIKE A **SEED.**

PICKLES
AND
PRAYER

By Bethany Marshall
Illustrated by Sarah Vogel

WE **PLANT** IT DOWN,

BECAUSE WE KNOW OUR **NEED**.

FAITH CAN TAKE SOME **TIME** TO **GROW**,

BUT AFTER A **WHILE** IT STARTS TO **SHOW**.

8

LIKE A PLANT,
OUR PRAYERS GROW STRONG.
ROOTS GROW AND VINES REACH,
HEALTHY AND LONG.

Soon a bud,
and then the
FLOWERS!

We hope for **MORE**
and **MORE** spring **SHOWERS!**

IT WON'T BE LONG
UNTIL THEY'RE HERE:

11

Fresh cucumbers

TO MAKE **PICKLES,** MY DEAR!

13

WHEN WE **PRAY**

WE SEE A **PROCESS,**

LIKE **PLANTING**, THEN **WAITING** AND **WATCHING** THE PROGRESS.

AS WE **PRAY,** GOD KNOWS OUR **NEED.**

SO **TRUST** AND **HOPE**

—JUST LIKE A **SEED!**

WHEN IT'S **TIME**
IT WILL **GROW**,
AND IN THE
RIGHT SEASON
IT WILL **SHOW**.

PICKLES AND PRAYER
ARE ALL YOU NEED;
JUST REMEMBER,
IT'S LIKE A SEED.

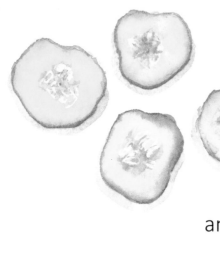

A Pickle Prayer

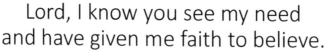

Lord, I know you see my need
and have given me faith to believe.

Let your will be done today
in hearts and lives of people, I pray.

Lord, your love is big and strong,
it's big enough to carry all of us along.

You give me patience while I wait,
and I know what you're doing is great!

I will pray and never forget
that just like those seeds, my need will be met.

Amen.

REFRIGERATOR DILL PICKLES

These pickles taste so fresh and have just the right amount of dill and garlic. You can also cut the cucumbers into chips if you prefer a pickle chip instead of a spear. The pickles should be good for six weeks. Enjoy!

Ingredients:
3 1/2 cups water
1 1/4 cups white vinegar
1 tablespoon sugar
1 tablespoon sea salt
4 cups cucumber spears
2 cloves garlic, whole
2 heads fresh dill

Directions:
Prep: 10 m | Cook: 15 m | Ready in 3 days

Stir water, vinegar, sugar, and sea salt together in a saucepan over high heat. Bring to a boil. Remove from heat and cool completely.

Combine cucumber spears, garlic cloves, and fresh dill in a large glass or plastic container. Pour cooled vinegar mixture over cucumber mixture. Seal container with lid and refrigerate for at least three days.

Nutrition Facts: Per serving: 13 calories

- Fat: 0.1 g
- Carbohydrates: 3.1 g
- Protein: 0.4 g
- Cholesterol: 0 mg
- Sodium: 444 mg

About Bethany Marshall

Bethany is the founder and director of Daughters Conference, a conference birthed out of her heart for teenage girls. Bethany currently resides in Altoona, Pennsylvania, with her husband, Micah, and her bouncy boxer dog, Timber. Bethany enjoys drinking good coffee, shopping for good deals, and has loved pickles since she was a little girl.

About Sarah Vogel

Sarah Vogel is a self-taught artist, entrepreneur, and owner of The Clay Cup in Altoona, Pennsylvania. She and her husband, Jeremy, are foodies at heart and enjoy cooking and exploring new foods together. She primarily works in mediums such as watercolor, colored pencil, and ink. Her favorite subject to paint is one that everyone can relate to—food!